Introduction

For being 35 years old, people say that I have achieved a lot in my life. I don't really see it that way. The past, to me, is a source of knowledge. And not being too attached to it allows me to see it for what it is.

At 18, I was one of the youngest elected 'first successors' in Belgium. I managed to spark a great deal of discussion around discrimination with my decision to participate in Big Brother. I wrote a book when I was 21 years old and started a protest movement around mandatory voting in Belgium at the age of 25. I became a world-record-breaking professional gamer when I was 26 and capitalized on this with online videos that made me one of the first successful gamers on YouTube. At this point, YouTube was in its infancy and monetization was not yet possible. So I got into poker and turned 5 dollars into more than $300,000 in the course of one year. This was the result of persistent dedication, playing 16 hours a day, 24 tables simultaneously and at one point even managing to set the world record of playing one million hands in one month. I made several documentaries which reached millions of people and started my efforts on charity when I was 31, raising more than $20 million for children in need. This led to my appearance on many media outlets such as CNN, Fox, The Wall Street Journal, Bloomberg TV and others. I realize this can look impressive, but I do not derive any sense of identity from these accomplishments, because I know that if it was not for my environment at those specific points in time, I would be an entirely different person.

This book won't change your life but applying the insights will.

Chapter Zero

Later on in the book, you will get a better understanding of why I wrote Chapter Zero. The state you are in while reading this book highly influences how you experience and interpret it. This is the case for a lot of things in life. How efficiently you study, for example, is strongly dependent on how focused you are at that moment. Writing this book, I made everything very concise. If right now you are in a state where you find it easy to absorb and reflect upon new information, taking small breaks from reading on a regular basis can help maintain focus. If you aren't fully 'in the zone', I would advise to pick up the book at a later time.

Chapter I: Do We Speak The Same Language?

When we speak, we subconsciously assume that the thoughts and emotions we evoke in others are similar to those that are unique to our own experience. This misunderstanding is exacerbated when we use loaded concepts such as God, love or truth. As a result, people often have endless conversations where they talk past each other and end up disagreeing on things they don't disagree on at all and vice versa.

That is why I wanted to address this early on in the book. Depending on how good I am at writing, I can avoid miscommunication. But since English is not my native language, I wanted to explain the mechanisms so you can also be part of this process. The best way to understand what someone is trying to say is by first listening without bias and by trying to see things from the other person's perspective. Being aware of this in conversations can also enable you to explain yourself more clearly, as you'll tend to use the other person's framework to get your ideas across. Applying this every day and always seeking to adapt and improve when it comes to putting thoughts into words can drastically impact your social and professional life as well as expand your self-knowledge. This is a skill that takes time and practice as thoughts always start off as vague and abstract. Being able to put thoughts into words defines how we present ideas and beliefs to others but also how we give structure to our own thinking. Sharing ideas by using relatable examples can help and is often one of the better ways to get your points across.

Chapter II: Questioning Our Truth

It can be profoundly confusing to grasp the concept that there is no such a thing as an absolute truth. It is impossible to know whether your experience of reality is a simulation, a dream or a hallucination since seeing a 3rd party's point of view as an objective truth is an assumption within your frame of reference. This can sound counter-intuitive at first but the world you experience would not exist without you. Fully understanding this concept can restructure the brain to be less attached and more capable of rationally evaluating different beliefs.

The problem with seeing even our own existence as an absolute truth is that we have to assume that time and space objectively exist. Surprisingly, this is a point of quite some debate in science and there are phenomena that violate our intuitive understandings of them. When there is strong evidence, scientists consider a theory to be true, but only within our current knowledge or understanding of it. You don't have to take my word for it, questioning everything I bring up in this book is a good mental exercise that will help you correct flaws within socially conditioned beliefs.

I try to be very empirical and construct logical arguments that are based on the assumptions I deem likely, such as what I read in reliable scientific papers. Emotionally, it is very appealing to believe in absolute truths and most people tend to avoid or reject confrontational ideas because their gut feeling tells them to do so. But erroneous certainties can hold people back or lock them into beliefs that may be illogical or even harmful. Unfortunately, these beliefs are most often created by rationalizing around conclusions and decisions after they've already been made. And even though these automatic mechanisms are natural, we also have the ability to override them with self-awareness. Some might wonder why that even matters if, either way, there are no certainties without absolute truths. But instead of thinking with certainties, it is more accurate to think in probabilities. This is perhaps the most important insight I have learned from how scientists approach the smallest building blocks of our world. Our entire universe is made of quanta such as electrons and photons that all behave probabilistically rather than deterministically. Ultimately, anything is possible and answering any yes or no question with "there is a chance" is actually factually correct. As much as we'd love to believe in absolute truths, real answers will always lie in probabilities and approximations.

Chapter III: Conditioning: How Deep Does The Rabbit Hole Go?

When people think about conditioning, the overall perception is that it influences our actions but we are still in control. We have the tendency to ignore the impact of our environment when we look at ourselves and take many processes that have been fundamental to our development for granted. This ranges from the language we speak to how we define concepts or even the emotions we experience when we think about things. This then translates into our body language, our intonations and ultimately the culture we feel part of. All these processes are in one way or another conditioned and being aware of this can highly increase the control we have over ourselves.

There is an endless number of examples that can be given in relation to this topic and many of these can sound mind-blowing and hard to believe at times. Yet, these dynamics define our everyday interactions and decisions more than our own perceived level of control. Most of our actions and thoughts happen subconsciously and conditioning lays down the foundation of these processes as we grow up. We accept them as part of our identity and personalize them so we feel unique and special. Our sense of self has little to do with how we perceive it and more with how we have been molded by our environment. I found that neuroscience provides the best framework to master the self. Expanding on this, the following five chapters will be more scientific and less personal.

Chapter IV: The Brain & Neuroplasticity

The human brain is a network of approximately one hundred billion neurons. Different experiences create different neural connections and these bring about different emotions. Depending on which neurons get stimulated, certain connections will become stronger and more effective while others may become weaker. This is referred to as neuroplasticity. Someone who trains to be a musician will create stronger neural connections that link the two hemispheres of the brain in order to be musically creative. Virtually any sort of talent or skill can be created through training. Rüdiger Gamm for example, who was a self-admitted hopeless student, used to fail at basic maths and went on to train his abilities to become a famous mental calculator, capable of performing extremely complex mathematics.

Rationality and emotional resilience work the same way, these are neural connections that can be strengthened. But this also applies to negative thinking. It's possible to have two elderly people who may have had similar lives, yet one person is perfectly happy while the other is very unhappy and has a negative view on the same things. Everything depends on which neurons they have been stimulating throughout their lives. Whatever you are doing at any time, you are physically modifying your brain to become better at it.

Since this is such a fundamental mechanism of the brain, being self-aware can greatly enrich our life experience.

Chapter V: Social Neuroscience

Specific neurons and neurotransmitters such as nor-epinephrine, trigger a state that can be described as having an 'active ego' when we feel that our own thoughts have to be protected from the influence of others. If we are then confronted with differences in opinion, the chemicals that are released in the brain are the same ones that try to ensure our survival in dangerous situations. Sometimes debates go on endlessly because people keep expressively resisting differences in opinion. When we're in a defensive state, the more primitive part of the brain interferes with our rational thinking and the limbic system can even knock out most of our working memory, physically causing narrow mindedness. We see this in the politics of fear, the strategy of poker players or simply when people feel defensive and stubborn in discussions. No matter how valuable an idea is, the brain has trouble processing it when it is in such a state. On a neural level, it reacts as if our life is being threatened, even if the threat comes from harmless opinions or even facts that we may otherwise find helpful and could rationally agree on.

But when we express ourselves and our views are appreciated, these defense chemicals decrease in the brain and dopamine neurotransmission activates the reward neurons, making us feel empowered and increasing our self-esteem. Our beliefs have a profound impact on our body chemistry, this is why placebos are so effective. Self-esteem or self-belief is closely linked to the neurotransmitter serotonin. A relative imbalance of it often leads to depression, self-destructive behaviour or even suicide. Social invalidation is the primary cause of this while validation has the opposite effect: Social validation increases the levels of dopamine and serotonin in the brain and allows us to let go of emotional fixations and become self-aware more easily.

Chapter VI: Mirror Neurons & Consciousness

Social psychology often looks at the basic human need to fit in and calls this the normative social influence. When we grow up, our moral and ethical compass is almost entirely forged by our environment, so our actions are often a result of the validation we get from society.

But new developments in neuroscience are giving us a better understanding of culture and identity. Recent neurological research has confirmed the existence of empathetic mirror neurons. When we experience an emotion or perform an action, specific neurons fire. But when we observe someone else performing this action or when we imagine it, many of the same neurons will fire again as if we were performing the action ourselves. These empathy neurons connect us to other people, allowing us to feel what others feel. Since these neurons respond to our imagination, we can experience emotional feedback from them as if it came from someone else. This system is what allows us to self-reflect.

The mirror neuron doesn't know the difference between it and others and is the reason why we are so dependent of social validation and want to fit in. We are in a constant duality between how we see ourselves and how others see us. This can result in low self-esteem or a craving for attention as well as feeling that no one understands us or the urge to act against our own intentions for the validation of others.

Scans show that we experience these negative emotions even before we are aware of them. But when we are self-aware, we can alter misplaced emotions because we control the thoughts that cause them. This is a neurochemical consequence of how memories become labile when retrieved and are restored through protein synthesis. Self-observing profoundly changes the way our brain works. It activates the self-regulating neocortical regions which give us an incredible amount of control over our feelings. Every time we do this, our rationality and emotional resilience are strengthened. But when we're not being self-aware, most of our thoughts and actions are impulsive and the idea that we are randomly reacting and not making conscious choices can be instinctively frustrating. The brain resolves this by creating explanations for our behaviour and physically rewriting it into our memories, making us believe that we were in control of our actions. This is called backward rationalization and it leaves most of our negative emotions unresolved and ready to be triggered at any time. They become a constant fuel to our confusion as our brain will keep trying to justify why we behaved irrationally.

All of this complex and almost schizophrenic subconscious behaviour is the result of a vastly parallel distributed system in our brain. There is no specific center of consciousness, the appearance of a unity is in fact each of these separate circuits being enabled and being expressed at one particular moment in time.

Our experiences are constantly changing our neural connections, physically altering the parallel system that is our consciousness. Direct modifications to this can have surreal consequences that bring into question what and where consciousness really is.

If your left cerebral hemisphere for example were to be disconnected from the right, as is the case in split brain patients, you would be able to speak, talk and think normally from the left hemisphere while your right hemisphere would have very limited cognitive capacities. Your left brain will not miss the right part, even though this profoundly changes your perception. One consequence of this is that you can no longer describe the right half of someone's face. But you'll never mention it, you'll never see it as a problem or even realize that something has changed. Since this affects more than just your perception of the real world and also applies to your mental images, it is not just a sensory problem but a fundamental change in your consciousness.

Chapter VII: Our Will is in The Neurons

Each neuron has a voltage, which can change when ions flow in or out of the cell. Once a neuron's voltage has reached a certain level, it will fire an electrical signal to other cells, repeating the process. When many neurons fire at the same time, we measure these changes in the form of a wave.

Brainwaves underpin almost everything going on in our minds, including memory, attention and even intelligence. As they oscillate at different frequencies, they get classified in bands called alpha, theta, beta and gamma, each associated with a different task. Brainwaves allow brain cells to tune in to the frequency corresponding to their particular task while ignoring irrelevant signals in a similar way as a radio homes in on different waves to pick up radio stations, since the transfer of information between neurons is enhanced when their activity is synchronized. These mechanisms also give rise to cognitive dissonance, the frustration caused by simultaneously holding two contradictory ideas. Our will is merely the drive to reduce dissonance between each of our active neural circuits.

Evolution can be seen as the same process, where nature tries to adapt or resonate with reality. By doing so, it evolved to a point where it became self-aware and started to question itself. When a person faces the paradox of wanting purpose while thinking that human existence is meaningless, cognitive dissonance occurs. Throughout history this has led many to reach for spiritual and religious guidance, challenging science as it failed to give answers to existential questions such as why or what am I?

Chapter VIII: Who or What Am I?

The left cerebral hemisphere is largely responsible for creating a coherent belief system in order to maintain a sense of continuity towards our own lives. New experiences get folded into the pre-existing belief system. When they don't fit, they are simply denied.

To counterbalance this, the right cerebral hemisphere has the opposite tendency. Whereas the left hemisphere tries to preserve the model, the right hemisphere is constantly challenging the status quo. When the discrepant anomalies become too large, the right hemisphere forces a revision in our worldview or belief system. However, when our beliefs are too strong, the right hemisphere may not succeed in overriding our denial.

This can create a profound confusion when mirroring others. When the neural connections that physically define our belief system are not strongly developed or active, then our consciousness, the unity of all the separate active circuits at that moment, is going to consist mainly of activity related to our mirror neurons. Just as when we experience hunger, our consciousness consists mainly of other neural interactions for consuming food. This is not the result of a core self giving commands to different cerebral areas, all the different parts of the brain become active and inactive and interact without a core. Just as the pixels on a screen can express themselves as a recognizable image when in unity, the convergence of neural interaction expresses itself as consciousness. At every moment, we are in fact a different image, a different entity when mirroring, when hungry, when reading this text. Every second we become a different person as we go through different states. When we are mirroring, we may construct the idea of identity. But if we observe ourselves with our scientific understandings, we see something completely different.

The extent to which our neural activity brings about our consciousness, which creates our sense of reality, goes far beyond our current concept of the self. The separation we perceive between our environment and ourselves is only a conceptual practicality that we use to make sense of things. This is not a hypothetical philosophy, it's a logical consequence of how everything we experience, external or internal, takes place within our consciousness from a neural activity point of view. Seeing the concept of the self as merely yourself excluding the environment is a misconception.

This is even reflected in our super-organismal features through evolution, where our survival as individual primates relied on our collective abilities. Over time, the neocortical regions evolved to permit the modulation of primitive instincts and the overriding of hedonistic impulses for the benefit of the group. Our selfish genes have come to promote reciprocal social behaviours in super-organismal structures, discarding the notion of survival of the fittest. The brain's neural activity resonates most coherently when there's no dissonance between these advanced new cerebral regions and the more primitive ones. 'Selfish tendencies' is a narrow intellectual interpretation of what self-serving behaviour entails wherein human characteristics are perceived through the flawed paradigm of identity instead of what we are, a momentary expression of an ever-changing unity with no center.

The psychological consequences of this as a more objective belief system allow self-awareness without attachment to the imagined self and brings about dramatic increases in mental clarity, social conscience, self-regulation and what's often described as being in the moment.

The common cultural belief has mostly been that we need a narrative to establish moral values. But with our current understandings of the empathic and social nature of the brain, we understand that a purely scientific view with no attachment to our identity or 'story' yields a far more accurate, meaningful and ethical paradigm than our anecdotal values.

This is logical since our traditional tendency to define ourselves as imaginary individualistic constants neurally wires and designs the brain towards dysfunctional cognitive processes, such as labeling and the psychological need to impose expectations.

Practical labeling underpins most forms of interaction in our daily lives. But by psychologically labeling the self as internal and the environment as external, we constrain our own neurochemical processes and experience a deluded disconnection. Growth and its evolutionary side-effects, such as happiness and fulfillment, are stimulated when we're not being labeled in our interactions. We may have many different views and disagree with one another in practical terms, but interactions that accept us for who we are without judgment are neuropsychological catalysts that wire the human brain to acknowledge others and share ideas without dissonance.

Stimulating this type of neural activity and interaction alleviates the need for distraction or entertainment and creates cycles of socially constructive behaviour in our environment. Sociologists have established that phenomena such as obesity, smoking, emotions and ideas spread and ripple through society in much the same way that electric signals of neurons are transferred when their activity is synchronized. In a sense, we are a global network of neurochemical reactions and the self-amplifying cycle of acceptance and acknowledgment, sustained by the daily choices in our interactions, is a chain reaction that defines our collective ability to overcome imagined differences and look at life in the grand scheme of things.

Chapter IX: Free Will & Quantum Mechanics

Through quantum mechanics, I have learned to see reality differently and approach all things as probabilities instead of certainties. In a mathematical sense, anything is possible. As well as in science as in our daily lives, the extent to which we can calculate or figure out probabilities is determined by our intellectual ability to recognize patterns. The less biased we are, the clearer we can identify patterns and base our actions on reasonable probabilities. Since it's in our nature to deny ideas that do not fit into our current paradigm, the more attached we are to our beliefs, the less able we are to make conscious choices for ourselves. By observing this process, we can expand our awareness and free will.

It is said that wisdom comes with age, but with openness and skepticism, the key principles of the scientific method, we don't need a lifetime of trial and error to sort out which of our convictions may be improbable. The question is not whether our beliefs are right or wrong, but whether or not being emotionally attached to them will benefit us.

It is hard to speak of a free choice when you are emotionally attached to a belief system. The moment we are self-aware enough to realize this, we can let go and calculate the real odds of what will benefit us the most.

Chapter X: What Now?

The insights in this book are based on current research and just as much as our understanding of the world has changed throughout time, these insights and understandings that determine our actions can also change through time. With the Internet, it is easy to scrutinize the information presented. This is important as it keeps you adjusted to reality and allows you to calibrate towards the better version of yourself. I like this metaphor, because having your best self as a framework is a very practical and realistic measuring tool to compare yourself with. It is unique to each person without having to generalize what is best for people to do. Ideally, you want to align your actions with the best version of yourself at any time. It is better to define this best version based on scientific findings rather than emotional attachments. For example, if you don't mind smoking, yet you know it is better for you not to, then you could acknowledge that a better version of yourself wouldn't smoke. The same would apply to other habits you would consider to be bad. The extent to which you can overcome these bad habits will greatly define your personal growth.

Chapter XI: Where Do I Start?

Gaining control is a process that takes time and practice, just as getting in shape requires you to work out. Changing your state of mind to being more rational and present requires regular stimulation of the neural pathways responsible for bolstering reason.

How to go about it most effectively varies from person to person, so this list is more of a guideline. What is most effective is not always what works best on paper, but rather what works best for you. From my personal experience, the habits that require the least effort are the ones that are adopted the quickest. The easiest one I can think of is taking the right supplements. All it takes is ordering them and taking them regularly. Vitamin D3 at times when you don't have a lot of exposure to sun can help a lot. Other supplements that are good to take include omega-3 and vitamin B-complex. This is what has worked best for me, but shouldn't be seen as a universal example. The effect of supplements and food is different for each person. I also take noopept, a popular nootropic, in combination with citicoline, which has highly improved the quality of my sleep. Depending on your lifestyle, these supplements might be more or less effective. Drinking coffee on a regular basis for example can greatly diminish the effects you experience from stimulating supplements.

Next on the list is working out, probably the most important one when I base myself on the feedback of my viewers. I know that healthy eating habits and a well-balanced diet can have an even bigger impact, but I am mainly looking at the habits that have the best chances to ripple throughout all aspects of your life. Everyone for example knows that eating healthily is good for you, yet it isn't something many people are aware of in their daily lives. Working out, on the other hand, has proven to be a great stepping stone towards an overall healthier lifestyle. That is why I mention it so early on, it helps you be more in control as it produces a better blood flow to the brain, resulting in mental clarity and increased self-confidence.

I know many might not have the will to go out and exercise even if they would want to. If you can't find the energy to do so, finding a friend to do it together with can help. If you can't think of anyone, my suggestion would be to use the Internet. If you live in the U.S. for example, you have websites like exercisefriends.com that allow people to connect for these types of activities. Working out is a big catalyst for a lot of other positive lifestyle changes and that is why, for people who don't work out, the chances of taking up the advice is lower than for those who do.

Next up is surrounding yourself with people that inspire you rather than inhibit you. Not everyone has this choice, but the extent to which you are able to do so can have far-reaching consequences throughout your life. Some people go through the biggest life changes by just not hanging out with the wrong people anymore, which can be more impactful than any other advice I could give you. It is important to be aware and remind yourself that your environment is a big part of who you are. If you still live with your parents for example, becoming financially independent so you can live by yourself can be a big step towards intellectual independence. The majority of people grow the most the moment they have to make their own decisions and take responsibility for them. If you are still young and moving out is not possible yet, compromising in order to keep the peace while you are in this phase of your life would be my general advice.

Next up is eating habits. Avoiding consumption of refined sugar is one of the most impactful steps I can think of. This relates to soda, cookies, candy or even fruit juice. Drinking mainly water and avoiding alcohol, coffee and especially sugary drinks will be hard at first but as you get used to it, your quality of life will improve significantly. Same applies to the consumption of meat or dairy products. Most of this advice is supported by, among others, the World Health Organization and doing your own research into these topics can help you understand more of the dangers and benefits. Be aware that all gut flora is different and whether a specific diet is better or worse varies from person to person and the examples I have given so far are quite general. Eating food that is easy to digest can also help as well as preparing the food with fresh vegetables and taking your time when eating. I learned that proper posture and taking my time has taken care of many of my own stomach issues due to my high paced lifestyle. I do know this is not applicable to all settings but to me it was definitely worth it. Even if it required me to adapt my eating habits, it has made me more effective as it helps me feel better and think more clearly.

Next up is the importance of making time. I just mentioned it when it comes to diet but, when applied to all aspects of your life, it can clear up a lot of mental clutter. Self-reflection and meditation can also be useful in these regards. For many people I know, meditation has changed their lives. Apps like Buddhify, mainly the gratitude meditation in the sleeping category, set me at ease before falling asleep. These mental noise reduction habits add up in the long run when practiced regularly. They require already some level of awareness and that is why I haven't mentioned them earlier.

Last but not least is ensuring quality of sleep. Although this one ends up falling into place when adopting all these other habits that lower stress.

There are many self-help books that explain how to motivate yourself in doing all of this and while they sometimes work, I decided to focus more on the underlying dynamics that give you control.

Chapter XII: Why Do You Want What You Want?

We live in a heavily consumption-focused culture where having more and more is associated with success. So when people think about what they want, a lot of the time they want more than what they already have. You can wonder to which extent this is your own free choice if what you want is heavily conditioned by your environment. Analyzing the concept of freedom and evaluating how much it applies to us rather than letting it be defined by our conditioning allows us to reflect on our actions more consciously. But as long as we feel entitled, we have a hard time seeing our choices for what they are. We will more easily backwards rationalize to make it fit within our current paradigm since our will is mainly the drive to reduce the dissonance within our neural activity. Depending on what neural networks are active, your needs change all the time. A good salesman for example knows exactly which parts in our brain he has to activate to make us want something we don't want at all. This is just one example of how our perception of free choice is something we tend to rationalize afterwards. Self-awareness allows us to put our decisions in a larger context where our needs are perceived through a wider lens, allowing us to make more accurate decisions. This is probably one of the more powerful insights in this book. For example, there is no wealth in the world that you could want that would be more valuable than what you already have. Realizing this may make you value what you have a lot more.

This is quite present in spiritual beliefs such as eastern philosophy and can still be relevant in today's society. Not taking what you have for granted will benefit you more than the excitement from acquiring superficial things and will result in a more fulfilling and minimalist lifestyle. We still have more luxury than kings or queens a thousand years ago so it is just a matter of perspective. That is one reason why the gratitude meditation is so helpful to me. As times change and society gets more and more wealthy, the real richness comes from within.

Chapter XIII: What Do I Genuinely Want?

When you strip your self from all the noise and replace your concept of identity with a clear view on your core self, you achieve a state of clarity with little conflict that I could best describe as a choiceless awareness. What matters at that point is merely what makes sense and becomes similar for everyone. It may express itself differently from person to person but as the laws of physics are the same for all of us, they also equally underpin the processes of our biology. This can be illustrated by how two individuals growing up together are able to learn the same language. We are very alike and that is why applying reason to shared knowledge brings about similar action. In the end, what we really want comes down to understanding what we are. And most of these answers can be deduced from our biology. The urge to reproduce, for example, evolved into our need to find a partner. Figuring out how to connect our biological purpose to our actions is what matters. And since there is a clear line to be drawn from stardust evolving to us we just need to follow up on that to understand our design. It explains why we are here and is wired into every single cell. These are the same patterns that allowed stardust to ultimately question itself. When looking at these existential questions such as the meaning of life, we do so through our own subjective lens. We come up with personalized answers just as we come up with rationalizations to understand our emotions. But it is only by having perspective and looking at ourselves from a bigger picture, a grander scheme, that we can really pinpoint the answers. Understanding this will bring about a clear and scientific moral compass with values that transcend esoteric and spiritual beliefs.

Chapter XIV: Practical Application

If we apply logic and reason to our insights in order to determine our actions, choiceless awareness arises. You simply do what you have to do. This can sound confusing but when considering all the input that reality presents to us, determining the best course of action is a process that becomes very linear. Even when presented with different choices that are similar, choosing one rather than being stuck is more effective. These choiceless moments are omnipresent in our life but we don't experience them as such because we take them for granted. A mother taking care of her child for example, or having to go to the store to buy food are things we do naturally every day. Your actions flow out of your mindset without being paralyzed by the abundance of choice. Because if we look at things rationally and efficiently, much of the choices fade away. Acting upon common sense and adjusting these actions based on reality is a very simple mechanism we have lost track of, due to the overwhelming presence of distractions. You can see this with people in remote villages for example, who experience very little distractions as life is very simple to them. This then translates to more mental clarity and being in the moment.

Understanding the brain has been a big leap forward for humanity, however it takes time to propagate through society and to shape our psychological understandings of who we are. A lot of the insights in this book are based on recent studies and if it wasn't for these, I wouldn't be the person I am today. Nurturing your brain to be able to put these insights into practice is vital. The mind-body relationship I talk about in Chapter XI is an important stepping stone and knowing the importance of this relationship brings about quite some activities that people can start with today. What is even more important than knowing what to do is whether or not you will act upon it. The distance between knowing and doing can be substantial and it can take time for people to get there.

Chapter XV: The Right Mindset

While it might not be clearly defined, when we take a moment to think about it, we all have subconscious core values that we feel most connected to. Core values differ from person to person and can range from freedom and family to money or religion. As these subconscious beliefs define our actions, having a foundation that is factually accurate will automatically result in more mental stability and consistency. That is why having 'making sense' as your core value is the essence of this book, since reason is what gives us control over our otherwise impulsive decisions. It originates from the mathematical patterns that govern our reality and gives rise to the complex neural structures required for our thoughts or feelings to exist. That is why aligning our beliefs with these mathematical patterns creates a paradigm with little contradiction. Since all we need to do to reduce our inner conflict is find out how to make sense of it within the context of our reality. Understanding that on a fundamental level it is not you who is flawed but rather your beliefs leads to a high level of mental clarity and relief as all our fears and uncertainties suddenly become logical since we have the ability to explain them using neuroscience. We then either take action or come to acceptance with our dissonance rather than do what we usually do: beat ourselves up over it or create dysfunctional beliefs. This makes sense when we don't know that neurally emotions emerge before we can become aware of them. That is why applying reason to our knowledge is essential for making more sensible neural connections and why working out and eating healthily is so important.

Defining the right mindset in a universal and accessible way has always been a big challenge for me. And what has worked best so far is boiling it down to adopting a simple belief wherein 'making sense' becomes our core value. This has to happen on a subconscious emotional level as this is where it replaces our current impulsive drive with an intuitive urge to make sense instead. Wiring this subconsciously, which is possible for everyone, turns making sense into a primal desire and has been the defining factor and common thread through all my achievements.

From here on out, I will be digging into more practical topics. Rereading this book from time to time can be very helpful. The first two topics aren't as relevant but I included them since they are what people talk about most on my livestream.

Topic I: Religion, Politics, War and Compromises

Compromising on the quality of your message can allow you to reach a wider audience and finding the perfect balance can be difficult. The media, for example, has to constantly balance between sensationalizing their articles while at the same time staying close to the facts. If we are more emotionally driven, we tend to lean more towards sensational topics because they provoke stronger emotions. This also happens when we talk about politics as it is a lot easier to point fingers than being in charge of the policies ourselves where you have to make a choice between the lesser of two evils and no matter what you choose, you end up taking the blame. There are a lot of studies on how to increase the efficiency of a society but applying these theories to reality tends to be quite a challenge. There is a lot of corruption in politics and swaying public opinion to push one's agenda is often easy to achieve if there is enough funding behind it. It is not black and white though and we have come a long way. Take war for example, nuclear weapons have brought nations to a point where war between them would lead to mutually assured destruction and force us to resolve conflicts differently, resulting in the level of peace we experience today. And while almost everyone is against war, you don't always need much to sway public opinion when fear tactics come into play. Sometimes you don't really have a choice though as humans are capable of doing horrible things to each other.

We tend to have very polarized views when it comes to religion. The issue at hand is not so much what someone believes but rather to which extent they are radical about it. The Backfire Effect tends to make people more inclined to further reinforce and impose the beliefs that they hold. This has been demonstrated in psychological tests; when we are faced with counter-evidence for beliefs that we are attached to, our convictions are often strengthened rather than weakened. An accepting approach is statistically more likely to make people open up. That is why it is better to value people based on their actions rather than their beliefs. Because every belief has a mixture of good and bad and the real danger is when we start to see our way of thinking as the only way. After all, whether our paradigm is mainly religious or scientific, there is no such a thing as an absolute truth.

Topic II: Technology, AI, The Future and Aliens

Technology shapes us more than anything else. It makes us adopt new paradigms at a very fast pace and has become fundamental to our society and evolution. This all happens seemingly naturally, which is interesting considering that the influence of technology is not so much in our awareness. This doesn't mean that we aren't lagging behind when it comes to accepting new technologies. We can easily perceive it as a threat to our current paradigms but sooner or later we catch up because technology is just like reality, our beliefs cannot override it and we have to adapt at some point. One example that comes to mind is when cellphones became mainstream and making phone calls in public places was frowned upon, while this behaviour is now normal and omnipresent. Without us noticing, culture is slowly being shaped by technology. And what we've experienced thus far is only the beginning. Drones, robots, virtual reality, augmented reality, nanotech, bio-engineering, 3D printing and more, all these revolutions that are in front of us will already redefine the ways we go about our lives and how we see the world in just the next decade.

One popular topic is artificial intelligence and the fear of it being a threat to humanity. We have already been merging with technology for centuries. Glasses, for example, are a piece of technology that we use to enhance our vision. We're inclined to perceive the environment as separate from our identity but if we look at ourselves through the lens of technology rather than from our own perspective, the environment looks a lot more like it is fundamentally intertwined with us.

So let's assume we create artificial intelligence, will it end up destroying us? This is similar to how we like to think about aliens, in the sense that we make the error of approaching these questions from our own intellectual framework. If artificial intelligence would be more advanced than us, it would have an easier time overcoming our flaws. And when we think about the lack of a moral compass, it is because we see this in humans. But just as much as a moral compass was fundamental to our survival, the same would apply to AI. It is the same reason why countries with nuclear weapons don't engage in all-out war with each other. Being backwards compatible in culture and values measures the extent to which a society has evolved and benefits progress. The wider our intellectual awareness, the more we take care of the weaker. That is why I think it is more likely that AI or advanced aliens wouldn't destroy us since the need for and fear of destruction are human flaws.

If we base ourselves on the Drake equation, it is extremely unlikely that we are alone in the universe. One of the explanations for why we haven't encountered intelligent life yet is The Great Filter. It is a term coined in the Fermi paradox that states there is a filter that prevents life from reaching a higher level of intelligence. This great filter can either lie in the past or in our future. The former would mean that evolution towards intelligent life is the threshold while the latter would imply it is highly probable that self-destruction is inevitable.

It might also be possible that we haven't detected intelligent life yet because we have only been transmitting radio signals ourselves for about a hundred years. And if we look at how far we have come in this time span, it wouldn't be surprising if we would discover a more efficient medium of communication that we don't know yet.

On the other hand, it's statistically likely that advanced alien life would be millions, if not billions of years ahead of our evolution. As our own technology has come to a point where NASA is conducting research into the manipulation of space-time with so-called 'warp field' experiments, it might not be far fetched to assume that advanced alien life would have mastered the inner workings of time and space. My viewers love to talk about these sensational topics and while I always try to focus on what is relevant to them, I do spark their curiosity sometimes by theorizing about the singularity. A hypothetical moment in time where some scientists believe we will fully merge with technology and advance exponentially. When it comes to speculation about aliens, you can plausibly hypothesize the craziest things. Like for example that aliens might already be here and that the singularity is merely the point at which we merge with them. Not that any of this is actually relevant. That is why I rather focus on topics that really matter to us.

Topic III: The Importance of Rhetoric

Rhetoric is the art of constructing arguments and counter-arguments. If you are not adept at rhetoric, you can more easily be intellectually subdued. If you talk to someone about a specific topic and the other person's rhetoric is more advanced, you are likely to fall short of finding ways to counter the arguments. And even though questioning your beliefs is important, if it is not the insights or facts within the arguments that convince you but rather the rhetoric, it can lead to adopting flawed beliefs. This works especially well when the flawed beliefs are easier to live by.

On the other hand, being very competent at rhetoric yourself can also be a danger. If you are unaware and use it to shield yourself off from other people's beliefs, you might take advantage of a flawed argument someone gave you to dismiss everything this person has said, even if points were made that you could learn from. Another risk of having a strong rhetoric is that you have an easier time claiming the higher moral ground with how you are able to frame things. This gets people to validate you intellectually, making it easier for you to feel at ease being passive. In the end, actions speak louder than words. As long as you are aware of this, you will prefer to lead by example rather than winning debates.

Topic IV: What Questions To Ask

Most of the time, by asking ourselves the right questions, we unravel the underlying motives of why we ask ourselves the wrong questions. This is an important process because these questions plant the seed for many beliefs that will define how we act and look at the world. Combine this with our tendency to easily get emotionally invested in our beliefs and we can avoid a lot of dissonance by making sure we asked ourselves the right questions. When we're young, we don't have the intellectual capacity to challenge our conditioning. But as we grow up we can course-correct a lot of the flaws by asking the right questions. Sometimes that's all it takes, answers aren't even needed.

Here is a personal example of a question that has been responsible for quite some inner conflict when I was younger: Why care about the world if every action is inherently selfish? With all my logic, I couldn't find a satisfying answer up until a decade ago when I learned about the brain and understood that you have to define the concept of 'self' before talking about selfishness. And as already explained in the neuroscience chapters, everything we experience takes place in our consciousness and the 'self' encompasses more than just our flawed concepts of identity. While this entire train of thought started with a question that could have potentially led to the justification of egotistical behaviour, it should have started with me asking "What is the self?".

This also relates to many of the existential questions we have such as whether there is life after death. An even more important question to ask first is: What is time? Does time even exist? Because if the flow of time would just be an illusion of consciousness, then there is little use to wonder about the afterlife. For all we know, everything might be taking place simultaneously in a timeless now and time is merely a byproduct of perception.

Certain questions can also paralyze you as you become fixated on trying to solve them, such as "What do I do with my life?". This is a difficult question since it makes you look at your entire life with the limited information you have right now. It is very hard to predict the future and most of the time in life, one thing leads to another. The current moment can be very simple and being aware of that can be very relieving. A more efficient way to deal with these types of questions is to make the best out of the information you have now, since it makes you more capable of adapting to all the unknowns being thrown at you.

Topic V: Being Efficient and Effective / Result-Oriented vs. Outcome-Dependent

Being result-oriented is important as it allows you to measure your efficiency. But as with everything in life, most of the time it comes down to random events. You can make the most calculated decisions and things can still turn out for the worse, and vice versa. You can play the lottery for example and win, thinking you did the right thing. But being outcome-dependent is a very different mindset than being result-oriented. Ultimately, the outcome shouldn't matter and the only relevant factors are the knowledge at that point in time combined with your reasoning. We can learn things from an outcome such as how to optimize our workflow but it shouldn't affect us emotionally. When I reflect and look back at my decisions, I won't regret them if I did the best I could with the information available to me at that time. Being result-oriented rather than outcome-dependent allows you to achieve a very peaceful state of mind as it contributes tremendously towards mental stability and focus.

Evaluating your beliefs at all times is quite important as well. New research is being published all the time and there is no shame in improving your belief system to align it more with reality. As mentioned in the neuroscience chapters, we have the tendency of being emotionally attached to ideas, which limits our growth. There are studies about close to anything and doing research in the topics you deem important can greatly increase your effectiveness. You might wonder why being effective is so important but if it wasn't for nature being as effective for example, consciousness might have taken another billion years to emerge through evolution, if it would arise at all. Same applies to making money, if we could earn twice as much without any negative side-effects, why wouldn't we do that instead? The drive to be as effective and efficient as possible has been the foundation of my achievements and mastering this can enable anyone to do the same. This has been an ongoing process that I try to improve on every day.

Topic VI: How To Have The Biggest Impact

Having the 'biggest impact' means different things to different people. Some may see their biggest possible impact as ensuring that their children grow up with more opportunities than they had themselves, others may think along the lines of eradicating polio or creating new technology that turns sewage sludge into clean drinking water. Despite all of this being relative, there is an effective common ground for how to go about achieving what we want. The more logical you are, the higher your chances of success and by systematically learning from your mistakes and from the knowledge at hand, you can greatly speed up the process in getting better results. There is always a chance that random events slow you down and that, if you would have done it differently and less effectively at the time, the outcome would have been better. But that kind of reasoning after the facts is like saying it would be better to play a bad starting hand in poker after you have seen the cards on the table. It all comes down to making the right decision with the information and odds you have at that given time.

Having the biggest impact for me means moving forward in the broadest sense of the word. The way I try to frame it is by understanding how stardust evolved and eventually gave rise to consciousness. While vague, it has a clear direction and points towards a rich future of ever-advancing technology. My actions are just my best guess at adapting myself to the challenges that are being thrown at me. While this is personal, the more general answer I give when people ask me how to have the biggest impact is to first put themselves in the best position to improve one's mindset. Working out, eating healthily, taking the right supplements, meditating, proper sleep, putting yourself in an environment that stimulates you, reducing the mental clutter, then becoming financially independent and looking for like-minded people to make the biggest positive impact you can think of in relation to the situation you are in. For many, making a big difference in the world starts by becoming financially independent and your mindset is key in achieving this efficiently. After that, you will be in a better position to figure out what to do and how to put this into action. Having like-minded people in my environment has been essential to me. I know this feedback is a bit broad but since everyone's situation is different, making my advice too specific would reduce the chances of it being applicable. You have to find the best way to combine these insights and apply them to your own reality. I know how important personalized feedback can be and that is why I livestream regularly on twitch.tv/AtheneLive. For some, I even provide internships but I don't know if this will still be the case by the time you are reading this book. If you are still curious though, feel free to drop by on the livestream.

Topic VII: How To Become Financially Independent

This is one of the questions I get asked frequently and it's a hard one to answer. It highly depends on your mindset and the situation you are in. But most that do have the right mindset would have already tackled this issue because taking initiative and being analytical tends to solve problems naturally. Thinking in solutions rather than problems and being creative with what you have is what allows you to take advantage of opportunities that arise. I did it for example by selling online game currency when I was 19 years old and by playing online poker when I was 28. After that, I started making a living through advertisements on my YouTube channel. This is very specific though and would not work as well any more.

Having the right mindset is explained in Chapter XV and is crucial to being more effective and efficient. It starts by having a clear mind and has been mentioned several times so far. It requires mental and physical effort but will benefit you greatly in all areas of life. If you lack the mental clarity, you will also lack the self-awareness that gives you control and allows you to overcome your impulsive nature. Using myself as an example, I wouldn't have been able to turn $5 into $300,000 by playing poker if I was emotionally invested as that is what makes the difference between a losing or winning player. The same applies to stock trading for example. It requires a strong detachment from the invested money so you can make rational decisions based on statistics. If you let yourself get carried away, no matter the advice I give, it won't help much.

I experienced this the hard way when I wrote an educational software program to help my viewers make money playing poker on low stakes tables. While it explained step by step how to have an edge on these micro stakes tables, many failed to make a profit. I could have written a simple bot program that follows exactly these rules and would have made a profit, it was not so much the strategy that was the issue but rather the mindset. Same goes for tips about the stock market, there are so many books explaining how to do it and most traders still lose money. That is why working on your mindset as summarized in the chapters of this book will do more than any tips I can think of. I do understand that this answer can sound unsatisfying and that is why I will try my best to give some additional practical advice.

You can more easily become financially independent by having a more minimalist lifestyle. Even when grinding a low paying job, you can save up quite a bit until the point you have enough to not have to care about money all the time. With your mind being more at ease, you will be in a better spot to explore what you can do from there on. This also applies to your mindset, because living a minimalist lifestyle can be hard with the constant social conditioning that steers you to consume all this stuff you don't really need.

Your situation is also an important factor. If you have friends or family that can help you get a well paid job, you can make use of that. I would say that networking is becoming more and more important when attending university since so many jobs require experience and knowing the right people often gets you further than having great grades. If your parents are rich and don't mind helping out, you can save up quite a bit before leaving home. Many young people tend to not care so much about their finances until they have to take care of themselves and are in a harder spot to do so. Thinking about the real world and preparing for it when you are younger can make your life a lot easier when you grow older. Since you won't have to worry as much, you will experience less overall stress, which helps in making more rational decisions that enable you to become better at making money.

A few other practical tips. There are several websites that allow you to make money online such as for example leapforce.com and appen.com. I would also suggest checking out 'quick macros', it's simple software that allows you to record your actions on your computer so you can replay them afterwards. If you have a desk job for example, I would highly recommend it since it can make your life a lot easier and isn't that hard to learn. Just click record, do your stuff and replay it as much as you want. Understanding the code is quite simple and it's easy to make tweaks and optimizations. This has been a handy tool that has helped me a lot.

In contrary to developing the right mindset, these practical tips are not timeless. I don't know if they will still be of any use when you are reading this book but I hope they help.

Topic VIII: How To Prevent Procrastination

Many books have been written about this subject. From my experience, working out and eating more healthily will help you the most. This can be perceived as a paradox if you feel too lazy to work out or adjust your eating habits but it is important to know that you are not lazy, you only feel lazy. People have the tendency to label themselves and then act upon it as if it is a part of their identity. We illustrated throughout the book how identity is not what you are. No matter how hard it is to believe, you have great potential. Neuroplasticity is an amazing property of the brain, as discussed in Chapter IV. If you can't find the energy to kick yourself in gear, you can try to find someone to go work out with. For a better diet, you can put yourself in an environment where you can only choose from healthy foods so you can't be tempted. Refined sugar, for example, has a strong numbing impact on the brain. And while it's hard to stop eating it, it's the one thing my viewers were surprised the most about how much it did for them. It is quite difficult to avoid though because it is added to a lot of foods. Having a vegan diet can also help for some, as can taking supplements. But when it comes down to specifics, it is much harder for me to give guidelines. There are studies showing that it differs from person to person due to how complex and personal our gut flora are. Although some foods such as refined sugar are bad for everyone.

A healthy body goes hand in hand with a healthy mind and helps a lot at developing a better mindset. Picking up these habits will give you more energy which leads to more action and willpower. This can also fix the problem of boredom, which is often a side effect of being passive. If you are in a spot where you can't find the energy, don't dwell on it and try your best to break the cycle. After the first step it only gets easier.

Topic IX: Depression From Another Perspective

Not understanding the underlying neurological dynamics of depression can create a vicious cycle of anxiety as you may see it as a permanent problem rather than a temporary one. This triggers post-rationalized beliefs that can evolve into suicidal tendencies. People that have considered suicide at one point in their lives always look back with a sense of relief as they understand that depression is something you are able to recover from. Survivors who jumped from the Golden Gate Bridge in the US say what went through their minds the moment they jumped is how every single one of their problems was suddenly solvable except for the one they had just created.

Fortunately, I haven't had to go through depression myself. Outsiders sometimes rationalize that it would never happen to them but that's because they are underestimating how conditioning and environment can mold you. As an outsider, detaching yourself from your story makes it easier to be less judgmental as you start looking at depression through their lens rather than yours. This same awareness can be used to put your own problems in perspective as well. It does require a certain level of rationality and mental clarity though, which is harder to attain when we are in an emotional state. Saying that most personal problems in our society aren't real compared to other problems can make people very upset. It makes it look like there is no understanding for their situation even if what is said might be true. It requires perspective to stop taking things for granted and to be able to experience a sense of relief and peace as a result of this awareness. Imagine for example how devastated you would be if you'd receive a phone call about a close family member dying in a car accident. But if you would then discover that there's been a mistake and your family is still alive, you would be ecstatic even if in reality nothing has changed. We have the tendency to take the people we hold dear and what is most important in life for granted.

That is also why one of the most successful therapies for depression and even schizophrenia has been to let patients take on a role wherein they have to help others. It moves neural activity away from what's keeping negative fixations alive and shifts it towards the mesolimbic reward pathway, which also lights up when we experience pleasure such as having sex or enjoying great food. In addition, fMRI scans show that the brain is sensitive to whether we are being purely selfish or contributing to the lives of others. As long as we feel that what we're doing is right, happiness and fulfillment are almost automatic. It makes a lot of sense when you think about it, yet makes you wonder how helping others has become a therapy. It is mainly the current culture and social conditioning that has made us lose track of what we are and what we are designed to do. You won't hear me complain though, if helping others is promoted as a way to get rid of depression, it is an additional way to stimulate people to help the world move forward.

This is just one of many treatments for depression and doesn't work for all kinds. Some are depressed because of a chemical imbalance in the brain. One of my better friends, a very stable and happy person, used to have moments where he physically couldn't find the energy to do anything. If this dragged on for a few weeks, it brought him to the brink of depression. As he couldn't find the psychological cause, he visited many doctors to take different blood samples and figured out it was a vitamin D and zinc deficiency. After supplementing these for a week, it fixed itself. Of course this doesn't apply to everyone but it illustrates that depression can have biological causes and is not always related to the psyche. It's impossible to cover the entire spectrum of causes and having your blood taken to analyze deficiencies can come in handy. Asking yourself questions to narrow down the underlying problem can also help in finding the cause. There are many foods such as refined sugar or junk food that can drain your willpower in life. I even know someone whose depression was caused by an old, leaking dental filling. That is just to say that you can not generalize the cause of depression and that sometimes the solution can be as easy as finding the root of it. If you don't find it though, it can stay a drag no matter how much you reflect on it.

In the end, having the right mindset can dramatically lower the chance of getting depressed since efforts to ensure a healthy lifestyle and helping others are more aligned with the current scientific understandings of what we are.

Topic X: How To Deal With Loneliness

It's a basic understanding of evolutionary psychology that we evolved to be social organisms. Just as surviving as an individual required us to evolve to want food or the need to reproduce has made us evolve to want sex, the need to survive as a species has made us evolve to want social contact. It is fundamental to our existence. This is the underlying reason as to why we experience loneliness. We tend to forget this since culture has evolved so much faster than our biology. The extent to which we depend on each other for survival has diminished a lot in modern society, yet our biological social needs haven't been able to adapt as fast. The disconnect here is why loneliness is so common. People in developing countries tend to experience this less as they need each other more.

If it was just a matter of knowing and understanding this, it would be an easy issue to overcome. We would just hang out more and make friends. But the problem gets more complicated when you add social conditioning to the mix along with flawed paradigms built upon our concepts of identity. We easily tend to simplify our perception of others by categorizing people as good or bad based on our own experiences. Bit by bit, we end up isolating ourselves since there is little room for human complexity in such a worldview. If you are surrounded by people who think that way, you might try and fit in but the best thing you can do is seek out others who are like-minded. Unless this is how you look at the world as well, the best thing you can do then is re-evaluate your paradigm. Many people don't know any better because it is how they grew up and that is why reflecting on these insights can be very important.

If we want to have good friends, we first have to understand what it is that makes people good friends. The quality of your relationship is defined by what connects you. If it is college, then friendships will fade away when you graduate. If it is gaming, they will fade when you don't have as much time to play games any more. This happens all the time, especially when you get in a relationship or start a family because what you look for in a friendship is what defines the strength of it.

So in most cases the reason why people are lonely is because it either reflects what they value in life themselves and translates to the quality of their friendships or because they cannot find people in their surroundings that are compatible with them. In both cases there is something you can do about it. Improving your mindset allows you to reevaluate what is important in life, which is more in line with what you are and will make you look for people that do the same. The foundation of your friendship will be more durable as what connects you will be much stronger. This can range from working out together to helping improve the world. On the other hand, if you can't find people compatible with you but you do have the right mindset, you would keep looking and go about it in a structured and effective way. From my own experience, the strongest connection that can bind two people together is a common purpose that you value and work towards.

It seems to always come down to developing the right mindset, which, if you think about it, makes a lot of sense. Being more aligned with reality has been crucial to our existence and it's reflected in all aspects of our lives, including loneliness. If our mindset isn't compatible with itself and we couldn't stand a version of ourselves for example, we can wonder why we don't solve this problem by first working on ourselves.

Topic XI: Who Should I Trust?

The extent to which I trust people is very connected to how hopeful I am about humanity. Whenever someone breaks my trust, it indirectly affects how I look at people. I have had many experiences in my life that could have resulted in me giving up on humanity. The problem is that by doing so, it can kill you bit by bit from the inside. From an evolutionary perspective, our purpose is very linked with others. If you would compare society with a human being for example, each cell in our body could be seen as an individual. And just as much as the design of our cells evolved to help us, our social needs and drives evolved to help society. If you then take away the trust in others from the equation, we disconnect ourselves from our larger purpose and partially from the reasons of our existence. That is also why some people feel like there is nothing to live for when there is no one they care for. Since this is greatly defined by how we look at ourselves, the best way I have found to cope with these experiences is by using myself as a reference. As long as I can still trust myself, others will be able to trust me and I don't have to lose hope. That doesn't mean we should start trusting everyone. Being naive can expose you and damage your outlook in life. The idea that you cannot trust anyone and it's everyone for themselves, on the other hand, can also greatly impair the ways you're able to look at life.

Topic XII: How To Deal With Romantic Relationships

Our evolutionary drive to reproduce is responsible for the ways in which we can feel attracted to one another. Understanding this is important as it defines, for a big part, gender dynamics. Looking at mankind's history thus far, we only very recently started breaking away from patriarchal social systems where for example men were in charge of hunting while women were responsible for the children. This resulted in biological traits that are still present today even while modern society is progressing away from it. This is reflected in relationships where dynamics are often to greater or lesser extent still directed by primitive tribal instincts. Our current paradigm doesn't take our evolutionary baggage into account and can bring about a lot of confusion, such as when men sometimes view women as only being attracted to 'assholes'. The problem here is not that girls fall for 'assholes' but rather that they have a tendency to prefer men who are confident as it is one of the evolutionary qualities that increased our odds of survival. A caveman who is less inclined to assert himself is more likely to put his partner and children at risk. When such mechanisms are present for a thousand generations, you end up with these features being written into our DNA. And since relationships speak mostly to the emotions in us, relationship dynamics will go hand in hand with primal needs that have developed throughout millions of years of evolution. These primitive biological layers don't get to change over a few hundred years and that is why it is so important to course-correct them with our rationality and insight. The extent to which we do this will strengthen or weaken the more advanced and intellectual parts of our brain, allowing us to act with reason rather than emotion.

From my experience, showing acceptance for irrational behaviour or behaving irrationally yourself is not the best way of building a long-lasting relationship. Making clear what it is that you look for in a partner and finding someone who fits this description rather than trying to change people afterwards can only benefit the quality of your relationship and also tends to spark more attraction. Knowing who you are and what you stand for and only compromising when it makes sense is something that sets strong boundaries from the start that help to quickly reveal whether or not the relationship is compatible with you.

Many of the issues in relationships are a consequence of these irrational instincts where we lack the understanding in ourselves or each other. Since you can easily write a whole book about it, I decided to keep my advice simple.

Topic XIII: How To Understand One Another Better

Since human beings are social creatures, communication is central to our lives. Being misunderstood is quite common and often leads to feelings of isolation. This is because we lack sufficient understanding of the underlying dynamics of communication. Many of these topics have already been mentioned briefly in the first part of the book. Instead of repeating what I wrote in Chapter I, I will assume it's still fresh in your memory so feel free to read up on it again.

When someone's awareness is fully consumed with trying to fit in, their interactions almost exclusively consist of taking turns and speaking without listening. This is the result of a 'fake' identity which may still manage to come across as appealing to the outside world but is very unfulfilling and 'empty' on the inside. The way someone communicates says a lot about the person and if you never listen, you end up being surrounded by people doing the same. Being aware of this can improve your ability to connect as you start listening more. Instead of using your own worldview when speaking, you start to understand the other person's worldview and are able to use that instead. It charms you when you put a lot of energy into trying to understand people and helps you to achieve a lot in life.

Communication is more about how you are perceived than about what you actually say. Realizing this will make you more aware of how to say things. This has been a key factor in most of my perceived success and also extends into my personal life, my professional life, media, politics, almost everything. You're also much more likely to persuade people by knowing how to speak to them rather than knowing what to say and this is a process that starts with listening.

Topic XIV: How To Deal With Social Anxiety

Social anxiety is an issue brought up by many of my viewers and is mainly the result of a lack of confidence. The good thing about confidence is that you don't need it to have it. This can sound paradoxical, but if you can come across confident even if you are not, people will start treating you differently which then results in real confidence. A quick Google search shows you tips on how to do this, some examples are good posture and smiling. 'Fake it till you make it' is a social hack that works similarly to inflating views or likes on social media. People tend to flock to things and personalities they sense to be successful and since faulty conditioning sets the framework for how this is perceived, it is an easy system to cheat. You can wonder what it's worth when you understand the underlying dynamics and start realizing how empty perceived success is. Being famous myself, I have come to experience this insight first hand. It is hard to bring this across when everyone makes you believe it is so important. If you value my words regarding this matter, I can tell you it is as fake as it gets.

Practice is important for growing confidence. Trying out these tricks can sound intimidating at first but can easily become a habit when you do it on a daily basis. You can also achieve similar results by working out as, aside from its direct biological mood-lifting effects, it makes you feel better about your body. Another method used by psychologists who specialize in treating anxiety is making you aware of the spotlight effect: the tendency to overestimate the amount that other people notice your appearance or behaviour. It makes sense when you think about it because just as you yourself don't spend all that much effort and time scrutinizing the looks and behaviour of others, same applies to the extent that other people are doing this to you. It is similar to no longer having the urge to speak as much when you become aware that other people aren't really listening. When we are trapped inside our head, we can easily lose perspective and care or worry about mental images that only exist in our own world. Being obsessed with the legacy you leave behind is another example. Over time, at best, people will remember a name. And even when we think about big names, no one really cares or knows the real person behind it. After all, the real self is the neural activity at any given moment which is only unique to you. Being aware of this makes people more sincere as actions become aligned with core values rather than expectations of others. Letting go of identity can greatly improve this process and can also help when dealing with anxiety.

Topic XV: Self-Esteem and The Core Self

People that don't have self-esteem issues will have a hard time identifying with this topic. The seed of self-esteem or self-love is normally planted when you are a child. Your parents or your direct environment have a big impact on this as you grow up. Depending on how much you may have missed affection and validation in childhood, you may suffer from a fundamental lack of confidence, possibly even to extents that make you question whether or not your life's worth living. This often results in the urge to create a strong identity to compensate. When people grow up and realize that their identity is a facade, they break down and are left with their core self which they experience as worthless and weak. An exercise that has worked for my viewers is to look in the mirror daily for several weeks and give yourself the time and space to value yourself. Doing so will, over time, bring natural confidence as a byproduct. Healthy self-esteem is the foundation of how you look at yourself and how you look at the world. It cascades into being more easily inspired and also reflects in your actions inspiring others around you. Doing this exercise can bring back to the surface aspects of your self that you have repressed and neglected throughout your life. You might start repeating the story in your head that you are not worthy or smart or cool enough, but that is not what you are. Your existence is enough to make you valuable. When realizing this, your self-esteem will grow and shift from a victim mindset to a validation seeking one. And once you have enough of that, you let go and realize you don't have to prove yourself to others any more. That is when you know you have built an emotional foundation on which you can start building an even stronger rational framework.

Topic XVI: How To Deal With Judgmental Behaviour

Judging or labeling people is a way to condense information. By doing so, we speed up the process of evaluating whether a person or situation is beneficial or harmful to us. This has been relevant to our survival, where quick decisions could make the difference between life and death. Today we still judge people with our first impressions and use labels to condense information more efficiently. The downside is that we can easily miss out on information by prejudging or generalizing others. Jumping to conclusions influences the way we listen and communicate and can disable us from seeing the full picture. In worst case scenarios it can lead to ignorance, racism and other forms of discrimination.

From an early age, we are taught to use labels and judgments to compare ourselves with others. It starts with our parents telling us to be as clever as our siblings or to get better grades than others and can lead to an inherent feeling of not achieving enough. This lack of confidence and trust in ourselves can easily bring about a fake identity with ambitious goals that are not ours. Socially conditioned beliefs that tell us how to be happy and successful are then fueled by a validation-seeking mentality that has us constantly comparing ourselves with others. We are better off though comparing with our own best version of the self. This brings about an awareness that motivates growth and is more in line with what we are. Seeing reality for what it is and giving people the benefit of the doubt enables us to grow towards our own full potential rather than trying to be like others.

Topic XVII: Seeing Things For What They Are

When we form an opinion, we tend to forget how much of it is constructed by our own experiences. People might share the same reality but see and live in different worlds. The ones that see reality more accurately will be more flexible and go through life more efficiently. Most of our cognitive biases, such as the spotlight effect, are related to the same idea. This also undermines how we deal with global issues such as child mortality where some can feel at ease with accepting it by attributing it to overpopulation for example. Even though one of the better ways to combat overpopulation is by actually reducing child mortality as it statistically makes families decide to have fewer children. I use this specific example because our ability to rationalize things using our own intellectual lens through which we see the world can separate us from reality or even make us act inhumanely. By looking at reality for what it is and realizing that these children might as well be our own, or our little brother or sister for example, we develop a better and more accurate worldview which brings about a clearer moral compass.

We can often find ourselves stuck in an impossible situation just to realize that the solution is right in front of us. We have the tendency to make things more complex due to all the concepts we are conditioned to apply to our perception. No matter how well constructed our paradigm is, reality will always set the rules. And by not imposing our worldview, we can save ourselves a lot of trouble. Once we start adopting this outlook, a lot of our opinions become irrelevant and what is left is a clear view on how to best cope with the reality presented. Instead of dwelling on past events, we start to let go and move on.

Topic XVIII: Freedom and Responsibility

When we think about the concept of freedom, we tend to forget about responsibility. When confronted, we like to say "I am free to do whatever I want" or "it's my choice". We often use this way of thinking to discard other people's arguments, even if there might be truth to them. The concept of choice and freedom to do whatever we want is not always applicable when it comes down to responsibility. A mother for example would have a hard time arguing that she has the freedom to watch TV at a moment where she needs to take care of her child. The extent to which someone has a responsible mindset directly relates to their level of knowledge and awareness since these are the two requirements for developing a better sense of responsibility. No one holds you accountable for example if a child is dying without you knowing about it. The situation changes though when that same child is in front of your doorstep and you are aware of it. I experience quite a lot of inner conflict when I think about this specific example and imagine this same child to be far away. To which extent am I responsible for them if I know I can do something about it? Most of the time it is counter-productive to point fingers and judge people regarding their sense of responsibility since ignorance tends to be the cause of their inaction. Treating people based on their potential inspires action more effectively than blaming them for what they do or don't do.

We tend to use double standards when judging others compared to when we judge ourselves. But when we apply this kind of skepticism towards being more aware of our own actions, we can become a significant inspiration to others.

Topic XIX: Are Our Actions Insignificant?

We know from basic physics that every single action ripples through society in one way or another. People tend to diminish their impact by looking at the bigger picture and rationalizing around it. Humanity can be seen as a super-organismal structure and as much as one cell in our body can look insignificant, all of them together bring about who we are. All of our actions are relative but everyone can have a significant impact in their life. How you scale this up to achieve more is something you then learn from experience. Most of the time, we lean towards conforming to the status quo and post-rationalizing justifications for our current lifestyle. However, this kind of outlook comes back around to us one way or the other. If it is not by ending up less healthy and focused due to our eating habits, then it may for example be by experiencing a strong lack of purpose as we've stopped caring altogether. Right action is central to who we are and is reflected in both the smaller and bigger things. Many people in the world for example work for less than a dollar a day. The difference between their children having an education and a better future can be as much as a few dollars. While one life might look insignificant on paper, it means the world to us if it is someone we hold dear. Using our ability to put our actions into perspective goes both ways since we cannot use the bigger picture to morally justify our inaction and apply a different rule-set for the ones closer to us. This is also why I do believe in the good in people because when we are personally confronted with the ability to do something good right in front of us, we tend to do so. But when it is further away, the way we go about our right action can be more impulsive. If we would all go about it in a more structured way, the world would look very different. It would be reflected in the way that we spend our time as well as the extent to which we support politicians and companies and their policies with our votes and money. We wouldn't have to compromise as much for the better or worse as it is easy to just stop caring altogether. But just as trust affects the extent to which we are hopeful, the extent to which we care is what gives us purpose. Having the right mindset allows us to understand this and inspires change that starts with ourselves.

Topic XX: How To Achieve Happiness

Pleasure and happiness are two different concepts. While pleasure refers to a momentary state of joy, happiness refers more to an overall state of fulfillment. You can be very sad for example and still experience the pleasure of an orgasm. These concepts are often confused with each other and can bring about pleasure-oriented habits that end up undermining our happiness. Life is about balancing the two and depending on how much perspective we have, you will balance happiness over pleasure. When you are younger, it is often the other way around. But this starts shifting as we grow older and become more responsible.

Happiness and mainly pleasure is very central to our society. This has a lot to do with our conditioning and is paradoxically also the reason why so many people end up being depressed. Happiness is not something you can work towards, it is rather a state you automatically achieve when you are fulfilled. The best way I can explain this is by using a metaphor: you can compare your state of mind with an orchestra. When everyone is in sync and in tune, you experience harmony. Each musician can be seen as an active neural network. Likewise, if you get hungry for example, the neural network that is responsible for consuming food becomes louder and louder until you eat something. This is similar for all other primal urges and also applies to our conditioned needs. If you want a new phone for example, it will manifest itself as a neural network that will also be making noise until you either get a new phone or re-evaluate whether you really need it. You can already see what the problem is when being fixated on happiness. Since happiness is automatic when you have a harmonious orchestra, just adding this fixation on 'becoming happy' adds a musician or active neural network that will bring about disharmony. You literally create a paradoxical vicious cycle of ever-growing inner conflict which can only be fixed by becoming aware of it. This is supported by studies that show how, as long as we feel what we're doing is right, happiness and fulfillment are mostly automatic. The same goes for studies showing that people chasing happiness are overall less happy. A popular belief that has caught on in the past few centuries is that the meaning of life is happiness, but the real meaning of life has little to do with happiness itself and more with what causes it.

Topic XXI: How Important Are Beliefs?

When we ponder reality, one basic assessment would be that everything happens automatically. When we drop something for example, it just falls to the ground and follows specific patterns. When we then try to understand these patterns, we can come up with mathematical formulations to predict them, which can then be used to our advantage. When we think about people, it is different. Even though we are governed by the same physical laws.

You might wonder what this has to do with the topic 'beliefs', but they are very intertwined. Our beliefs are the programs that help us understand the patterns that take place around us and using them to our advantage is what has increased our chances of survival. Since we are going about it in a more advanced and analytical way than other animals, we have gotten a huge advantage over them and that is why we have become the dominant species. We have mastered the ability of molding the environment to our advantage because of our beliefs.

The problem is that our intellectual and rational capabilities are only a recent development in evolution. Fundamentally we are still emotional beings because evolution itself has been quite a random process spread out over billions of years where instincts and emotions emerged to help us become more adaptive to our environment. It is only after we developed our more advanced neocortical brain regions that we began to develop more rational and structured ways of thinking. This advanced our overall evolution tremendously while our biology lagged behind. We carry remnants of our past and that is why emotions can still have us act impulsively, even if we know that doing the right thing can be much more beneficial to us. The gap between our emotions and our reason is mainly defined by how much we stimulate these individual parts of the brain. If it wasn't for our education and culture, we would still be cavemen. The very reason why we aren't is because of our beliefs. They give us a huge advantage and define the extent to which we have been perceiving ourselves as humane. Fully understanding this can have drastic implications for our current paradigm. In Chapter IX it is explained how we all have the tendency to be in denial, but our ability to understand this allows us to override it and gain control through the neocortical circuits of our brain. Through self-awareness, our reason has the ability to override our emotions. This is a process that takes time, but neuroplasticity shows us that the brain is like a muscle and we can train the parts that speak to our reason to overcome our denial. Having the right mindset comes down to just doing that, up until the point where you don't even experience conflict any more as your right action becomes automatic and choiceless.

We are living in a time where we have more knowledge than any of our ancestors and as this knowledge has brought about all the technology and advancement we see around us, mastering our ability to improve our beliefs on the fly without being emotionally invested in them is one of the most important insights in this book. I sometimes wonder what advanced artificial intelligence would look like if it would acquire the ability to improve its own hardware and software. But with our knowledge of the brain and our insights into the world, we are already in a similar spot. Our growth potential is enormous. The only obstacle is the ignorance that arises from our beliefs if we don't have making sense as our primary core value.

Printed in Great Britain
by Amazon